Jesus – Hope for Life

Jesus – Hope for Life

The Christian Aid/Hodder Lent Book 2002

Edited by Paula Clifford

Hodder & Stoughton
LONDON SYDNEY AUCKLAND

Contents

Contributors

Inderjit Bhogal is a Methodist minister who held the office of President of the Methodist Conference from 2000 to 2001. He is Director of the Urban Theology Unit, Sheffield, and a trustee of Christian Aid. He ministers with a small congregation in an inner-city housing estate, and is particularly interested in immigration and asylum issues.

Paula Clifford is writer and Co-Publications Manager with Christian Aid. She has published books on a wide range of topics, the most recent being *Women Doing Excellently* (Canterbury Press, 2001). She is a Church of England Lay Reader in the Oxford Diocese.

Rebecca Dudley works part-time as Adult Christian Education Adviser at Christian Aid. She is also minister of Bethnal Green United Reformed Church. She lives in the East End of London with her husband and two children.

Eildon Dyer is Scottish denomination appeals and press adviser for Christian Aid. She is a member of Bert, a lay Christian Community in East Pollokshields, one of Glasgow's most multicultural areas. Community members are committed to staying in the area and supporting the local community. She has travelled extensively in developing countries.

Kathy Galloway is the Scottish Linkworker for Church Action on Poverty. She is a practical theologian, poet and liturgist, and a member of the Iona Community. She lives in Glasgow.

The Rt Revd John Gladwin is Bishop of Guildford and Chair of the Board of Christian Aid. He is the author of *Love and Liberty* (Darton, Longman & Todd, 1998) and has a long-standing commitment to making a Christian contribution to social justice. He is a keen beekeeper and gardener.

The Revd Dr Leslie Griffiths is currently the minister of Wesley's Chapel, Methodism's cathedral church, just outside the City of London. He spent the first ten years of his ministry in Haiti and was President of the Methodist Conference in 1994. He is an author and broadcaster, who loves presenting the challenge of Christianity in the secular postmodern age.

Garth Hewitt, singer, songwriter and author, is head of the London & South East Team of Christian Aid and Guild Vicar of All Hallows on the Wall in the City of London. He is also director of the Amos Trust. His most recent album is *Dalit Drum* (released through Christian Aid and ICC), produced with songwriter Paul Field.

Professor John M. Hull is Professor of Religious Education at the University of Birmingham and President of Christian Education. He lost his sight in 1980 and has described this experience in *On Sight and Insight* (Oxford, One World, 2001 reprint). His latest book, *In the Beginning There Was Darkness* (SCM Press, 2001) describes the Bible from the point of view of a blind person.

David Pain is head of Christian Aid's Churches team. With a background in adult religious education and community development, he has a particular interest in the processes through which Christians engage in social and political change. He attends the Quaker meeting in Oxford.

The Revd Dr Janet Wootton is minister of Union Chapel, Islington, a church that runs an extensive community and arts programme. She writes on liturgical development, and congregational and feminist theology, and is also a hymnwriter.

Introduction

Since Lent traditionally focuses on self-denial, penitence and suffering, the theme of *Jesus – Hope for Life* may appear to be a slightly unusual one on which to base a programme of readings for Lenten reflection. Yet the Christian message is indeed one of hope: not wishful thinking, but a confident belief both in our life with Christ to come and in the building of his kingdom in this life. Grasping that hope for ourselves and offering it to others is therefore a core part of our Christian discipleship.

The aim of this book is to explore in more depth where this hope lies; in love and forgiveness, in the breaking down of barriers and in the welcoming of outsiders, as well as the challenges it presents and the promise it offers.

Christian Aid seeks to offer such hope to people in some of the world's poorest communities, and this is reflected in many of the contributions to this book. The readings for each week in Lent explore a particular aspect of the theme of hope. Most, but not all, of these have been contributed by current members of Christian Aid staff. The weeks begin with a reflection for Sunday based on one of the 'I am' sayings of Jesus, and these are by outside writers with a close association with Christian Aid, as are the pieces covering Maundy Thursday to Easter Day.

I am immensely grateful to those of my colleagues who have spent precious time working on this with me, as I am to the distinguished writers and theologians from outside the organisation who agreed so readily to be part of this project. Each writer brings a slightly different perspective, and this has resulted in a book that I believe effectively combines the traditional Lenten disciplines of Bible reading and prayer with an opportunity to reflect very widely on issues that are of crucial importance to our world today.

Although the book has been conceived primarily for private use, to facilitate daily prayer and meditation, it could equally well be used as a basis for group study. The Sunday 'I am' reflections could provide a certain continuity for a group meeting weekly, and might be combined with a study on one of the passages discussed for that week. The prayers given for each day are also suitable for use in a group.

Jesus said, 'I have come that they may have life, and have it to the full' (John 10:10). May that be our hope throughout Lent, and may it impel us to be more effective in offering such hope to others.

Paula Clifford

Jesus – Hope for Life

Day I: Ash Wednesday

JESUS – HOPE FOR LIFE: INTRODUCTION
PAULA CLIFFORD

Baptised by John
Mark 1:4–11

As Jesus was coming up out of the water,
he saw heaven being torn open and the
Spirit descending on him like a dove. (Mark 1:10)

Jesus is the hope of human beings in all situations in life, however much these may appear to be devoid of hope. This is not simply a pious wish: our hope is grounded in the basic fact that God's Son fully adopted our humanity. Over the course of Lent we shall see how Jesus offered people hope in specific circumstances and continues to do so; but first we need to reflect on the hope that is inseparable from the nature of the Son of God. So in these first four days we shall see how Jesus took on our human condition, felt our tensions, shared our emotions, and experienced appalling suffering at the hands of people who despised him.

Mark makes it clear from the outset who Jesus was through the words of John the Baptist, a charismatic figure in his own right. John's Gospel also reveals Jesus' identity through a memorable theological statement: 'The Word became flesh and made his dwelling among us' (John 1:14). In seeking out John's 'baptism of repentance', Jesus reveals the full extent to which he has 'become flesh'. Although sinless himself, he aligns himself with sinners as he enters the Jordan. The consequences of his action quickly follow, as he is subjected to very human temptations. And much later, on the cross, he will experience a terrible feeling of being abandoned by God.

After Hurricane Mitch hit Honduras in the autumn of 1998, Pastor Felicito Gómez described how he met some of the survivors: 'They had absolutely nothing, nothing to eat, nothing to give their children. They were crying.' He added, 'To hear this, it felt like we were being stabbed in the heart . . .' A further poignant detail is that Pastor Gómez ministers at a church called 'The Church of the Way of the Cross'.

In his baptism, Jesus is showing his willingness to become vulnerable like Felicito and his congregation. Yet he is still God's Son. And as he undergoes this symbolic act of baptism by John, this identification with humanity, his Father announces himself 'well pleased' with what has happened.

'Thou who wast rich beyond all splendour, all for love's sake becamest poor.' Lord Jesus, we praise you that through your birth in Bethlehem and your baptism in the Jordan you shared our human condition. Help us this Lent to know for ourselves the hope you offer us, whoever and wherever we may be.

Day 2

Tempted as we are
Hebrews 4:14–5.6

For we do not have a high priest who is unable to sympathise with our weaknesses, but we have one who has been tempted in every way, just as we are. (Hebrews 4:15)

When Jesus was in the wilderness, the temptation he experienced, in three different forms, was to reveal himself through some dramatic act, which would virtually compel people to believe in him and follow him. But he knew that forcing people into faith is not God's way, and he remained resolute in his chosen path and purpose. We may not experience that particular temptation, but the message of the writer to the Hebrews is that Jesus suffered a conflict familiar to us all: the tension between doing what comes most easily and doing what we know to be right. It's a choice that faces many of us almost daily: between following God's way or doing our own thing.

The terrible slaughter and cruelty that took place during the 1994 genocide in Rwanda is still making the headlines. Yet not everyone turned a blind eye to the massacres and their consequences. Ernestine, now in her early twenties, was one of the many orphans who took refuge in the bush after their parents were killed. She was discovered by a soldier and taken to the capital where she now lives happily with the family of the soldier who found her. She attends a training centre along with other young people who were rescued in this way; they are cared for by soldiers or placed in foster homes.

The role of the Levitical high priest was to pass through the veil of the Temple, which was so dramatically ripped apart at the time of Jesus' death, to seek God's favour through sacrifice on behalf of the Hebrew people. Jesus fulfilled all that was required of a human priest – which included being able to 'deal gently with those who . . . are going astray', and being called by God. In addition, when he came before the throne of God, Jesus removed the barrier of the Temple veil, so that from then on all people could approach God directly. When we experience and give in to the familiar temptation to go our own way, it is in that breaking down of barriers that our hope of mercy and forgiveness lies.

Lord Jesus Christ, be close to us when we are torn between the way of the world and your way. When we are tempted, strengthen us; when we are alone in the deserts of our own making, protect us; and when we long for God, guide us gently into his loving presence.

Day 3

Compassion for us
John 11:32–44

When Jesus saw her [Mary] weeping, and the Jews who had come along with her also weeping, he was deeply moved in spirit and troubled. (John 11:33)

In St John's Gospel, the raising of Lazarus is the last and most powerful sign of who Jesus is before he is finally revealed as the Son of God in his crucifixion and resurrection. And this moment of major theological significance is also a time when Jesus tellingly reveals his own humanity. In the emotional scenes where Jesus' friends Mary and Martha lament their dead brother, Jesus shares their grief, not simply by taking part in formal mourning, but by shedding tears of his own for the loss that he feels as keenly as they do.

Commentators have noted that the word in verse 33 translated 'deeply moved in spirit' has connotations of anger in the Greek original. The suggestion that Jesus was annoyed that Mary and the Jews did not understand he had the power to bring Lazarus back to life seems debatable. Nor need we assume that he was irritated by their expectation of a miracle. Surely, instead, we can see in this something of our human anger when sickness and tragedy strike people close to us, particularly those still in the prime of life.

The human compassion that Jesus feels for his friends' suffering in the face of death is complemented by his divine power to restore life. And his prayer stresses yet again in this Gospel how Jesus and his Father are as one in all that they do, and in willing wholeness and healing for those who love them. These are firm grounds for Christian hope: a Saviour whose love for us is so great that he both suffers with us and with his Father offers us new life. In Tanzania a man called Johannes was dying of an AIDS-related illness. He was very poor and unable to feed his nine children. Yet as he approached death he discovered that dual hope of Christ-like love and compassion and the promise of new life. He said, 'The best thing in my life I waited for until I was almost dead. It has been the small Christian community in the village and the way we sing and pray together.'

Lord Jesus, help us to show to others the love and compassion you felt for your friends. May we trust in the hope you gave them of suffering shared and life restored, for ourselves, for people close to us, and for those who are unknown to us but loved by you.

Day 4

A servant like us
Philippians 2: 5–11

[Christ Jesus] . . . made himself nothing,
taking the very nature of a servant, being
made in human likeness. (Philippians 2:7)

For many people, humility does not come easily. We tend to prefer giving instructions to receiving them, and we take pride in our abilities and achievements. This need not make it impossible for us to exercise proper humility before God and other people, but it can make it difficult.

In becoming perfectly obedient to his Father, Jesus is the supreme example of true humility, both in setting aside the majesty of heaven for the inglorious earthly setting of first-century Palestine and also, once there, in being a nobody. He had to learn from earthly parents and teachers and be subject to the law of a foreign ruler, just like anyone else.

But this aspect of Jesus' incarnation is more than a lesson in humility. It is a further source of hope. In this passage there are echoes of the Suffering Servant depicted by Isaiah: the servant who was 'despised and rejected by men, a man of sorrows and familiar with suffering' (Isaiah 53:3). By replacing his 'very nature of God' with 'the very nature' or 'form' of a servant, Jesus is doing even more than accepting the human condition as we have seen it symbolised in his baptism by John. He was accepting without protest being despised by his own people and receiving the most terrible suffering at their hands.

Ana Vasconcelos used to be a successful lawyer in Recife, Brazil.

Then she took on work defending the rights of street children, and as she got to know some of the children her life was changed. She gave up her well-paid job and set up a hostel for vulnerable girls, which she now runs, to take children off the streets and to help them get some basic training. Ana's new life of service, with none of the status she once had, now offers real hope to young people living on the very fringes of society.

The hope for Christians the world over is that whether they are successful professionals or despised outsiders, Jesus, the giver of life, is there with them and is their inspiration, as we shall see as Lent unfolds.

'Show me your ways, O LORD, teach me your paths' (Psalm 25:4). Thank you, Lord Jesus, for faithfully following the way of service that took you to a criminal's death; and thank you for all those across the world who have obeyed your call to serve others. Teach me your paths, O Lord.

Day 5

FIRST SUNDAY IN LENT:
'I AM THE GATE FOR THE SHEEP'

JOHN M. HULL

John 10:1–10

He calls his own sheep by name and leads them out ... whoever enters through me ... [h]e will come in and go out. (John 10:3, 9).

This passage is about boundaries. A boundary encloses a space. There are correct and incorrect ways to cross boundaries. When a boundary is crossed incorrectly it becomes a barrier, and the result is confusion, but when a boundary is crossed in the right way, it becomes an open gate.

To a blind person like me, boundaries are very important. A closed door punctuates my space. If you open the door for me but say nothing, I may pass through without knowing it. Then I realise that I have gone too far. There should have been a door! Now I am not sure exactly where I am. In fact, I need to touch the door so that I can tell that I am about to enter. Boundaries should be respected.

In the same way, the kerb or the gutter marks the boundary between the pavement or footpath and the open road. I like a nice sharp kerb that I run my cane along so that I do not wander out into the road among the traffic. If there is a heavy fall of snow, and the curb is covered, it is hard for me to tell whether I am on the footpath or the road. Boundaries make for safety.

There is a boundary between the Christian faith and everything that is different from and incompatible with it. Without such a boundary the Christian faith would become indistinguishable. There would be no distinctive Christian discipleship, no clearly defined Christian identity.

At the same time, the boundary must not become a barrier. When the thief – the one who has no real understanding of Christian discipleship and wants to use Christian faith for some purpose of his or her own – tries to cross the boundary, it becomes a barrier. Only Jesus Christ, who is here called the good shepherd, can cross the boundary correctly.

The Lord of Christian faith crosses the boundary continually, and calls Christians to follow him. In this passage Jesus does not describe himself as a wall but as a gate, or a gateway. In other words, Jesus offers Christians both the clarity of the boundary and the freedom to cross the boundary. With this freedom, we go both in and out.

Lord, help us not to turn boundaries into barriers. Help us to exercise the freedom that we have as your followers; a freedom of exit and entry.

Day 6

CROSSING BARRIERS

EILDON DYER

Raising up the poor
1 Samuel 2:1–8

He raises the poor from the dust and lifts the
needy from the ash heap. (1 Samuel 2:8)

There are not many words of the Old Testament specifically attributed to women, so it is all the more significant that Hannah's prayer should be included. She had pledged to God that if he gave her a son she would consecrate him to his service. For a woman who had been tormented by her husband's other wife because of her lack of children, and then waited so long to have a child, it is hard to imagine her feelings when she gave up her child to God's work when he wasn't much more than a baby. A much more natural reaction would have been for Hannah to try to plead with God to keep him longer, or to have struck a bargain that he could spend half the year with her and half the year at the Temple.

But, like all good Jewish people, she had been taught to give thanks to God for everything and there is no sense here that she does so reluctantly: in fact, the very opposite is true. She is full of gratitude and praise to a great and mighty God who strengthens the poor and oppressed, and she includes herself in the list of those lifted up by God – the weak, the hungry, the poor and the 'barren'.

The people of Reunidas are currently singing of the greatness of God. At their regular services they give thanks for their dramatic change in circumstances. Now living in little brick houses with fruit trees around them, with cows they can milk, fish they can catch, these people of Brazil were once among the poorest in Latin America. Many of them have literally been lifted up from the dust and ash heaps. They were so poor that they made their living from scavenging on the city rubbish heaps.

The Movement of the Landless settled the people of Reunidas on to land they were legally entitled to, and now they have the resources to look after themselves and their children. They are not rich by Western standards, but their lives are transformed. One of them, Senhor Carvalho, says, 'This is paradise. Thanks be to God.'

God of the broken ones, the poor ones, the landless ones and the childless ones, we pray for the oppressed in our times. Bring about a world where the poor are given their seats of honour beside princes and use us as faithful disciples to work for that day.

Day 7

Respect for the poor
Deuteronomy 24:10–18

*You shall not deprive a resident alien or an
orphan of justice. (Deuteronomy 24:17, NRSV)*

This command to the children of Israel is part of a long list of
rules and regulations to make for a manageable and just
society. The poorest had to be looked after and workers had to be
paid every day on time. If not, and people did not have enough
money to buy food in the evening, the employers would be guilty
of misconduct. There is a strong sense in this passage that those
who had wealth and power were not to make the position of the
poor any worse. If a poor man had to hand over his coat as a
guarantee that he would pay back a loan, it had to be returned to
him at night so he would not be cold.

But perhaps what is most challenging is that these rules did not
just apply to the children of Israel themselves but also to the
'resident alien' – the foreigner, the immigrant, the refugee. Most
of these people had come to live in Israel either because they were
fleeing oppression elsewhere or because they were in debt. Today
they would be called economic migrants. And God is quite clear
that they are to be treated with justice and mercy.

We might be tempted to disregard this teaching because 'now
that faith has come, we are no longer under the supervision of the
law' (Galatians 3:25). But this theme of welcoming the stranger
runs as a theme throughout the Bible from Abraham and Moses,
to the prophets, and then to Jesus.

All over the world people are on the move and the Church has often been at the forefront of welcoming strangers. In Ghana, the Christian Council for Ghana has a programme for looking after refugees. People in Ghana are not rich, but the Church has responded in a Christ-like way. During the conflict in Kosovo, Serbian monks risked their own safety to shelter Albanians. In the United Kingdom, a country that is not poor and where our lives are not usually at risk, we too are challenged to respect the 'resident alien'. And respect is not charity; rather, it is about valuing people's culture, their faith and their skills.

Jesus, you knew what it was like to be a refugee, to be without family, to live among strangers and to be rootless. Help us to show your love and compassion to strangers in our communities and welcome them in the same way as you would want us to welcome you.

Day 8

When you give a luncheon or dinner, do not invite your friends, your brothers or relatives, or your rich neighbours; if you do, they may invite you back and so you will be repaid. But when you give a banquet, invite the poor, the crippled, the lame, the blind. (Luke 14:12–13)

Jesus used the experience of shared meals as one of many ways in which he broke down barriers and challenged social norms. There was a social etiquette about who would be invited to meals, and pious Jews were frequently scandalised by Jesus' audacious behaviour of eating with tax collectors and the poor. It is probably significant, then, that Jesus told this story while in the house of a leader of the Pharisees.

But this is not a teaching about good table manners or etiquette: it is one of Luke's many examples about how Jesus cared for those on the edges of society. Meals are intimate occasions and require time, money and planning, especially if you are having a banquet. When sharing a table, it is hard to escape people. There they are next to you helping themselves from the same shared pots and joining in the same conversation. After all the effort of preparing and planning a meal, it is nice to know that you may be invited back in return. But that should not be the motive, as Jesus tells us. We should include the poor because we want to, because we value them in the same way that Jesus valued them.

Jesus was also not telling people that they should exclude their friends. The form of the verb 'invite' in verse 12 implies that you make a practice of inviting, or habitually invite, only your friends. Friends are to be invited, but not to the exclusion of others. Perhaps this makes the passage even more challenging. It's one thing to have a meal for people you might find difficult. It's another to have your friends there at the same time and deal with their reaction as well. Christians in India have found verses like these utterly liberating. Many of them are Dalits, who are considered untouchable and polluted. People of a higher social class would never share a meal with them. Jesus offers them liberation here and now by challenging others to include them in the common everyday act of eating.

Lord Jesus, who loved to share meals both with your friends and those whom others found difficult, encourage us to find practical ways to include others in our lives. We acknowledge that it is often difficult to move out of our comfort zones, but help us to move forward in our discipleship.

Day 9

Giving sacrificially
Luke 20:45–21:4

*She out of her poverty put in all
she had to live on. (Luke 21:4)*

Jesus is weary and is sitting with his head down. Once again he has been berating the religious leaders about their hypocrisy. He could see that they were all show – strutting around and neglecting the important things in life like treating widows justly. Then Jesus looks up and sees one such widow who has become an example of true giving for all time, because when she gave, she gave generously.

In Jesus' time, widows were nobodies. Very often, without any means of material support, they themselves were the objects of charity. As we read in Deuteronomy, widows were to be looked after and treated fairly. The rich had to make provision for them. Jesus was unmoved in the Temple by the actions of the rich, but a widow shone out.

Temple rules at the time required that a minimum of two coins should be given into the treasury plate. What the rich gave, in effect cost them nothing. It made no difference to their lifestyle. They would still be able to afford to have decent meals and good clothes. The widow gave two coins that she needed to use to feed herself.

Such examples of generosity are repeated today and are potent challenges to the complacency and self-satisfaction of those of us who are well off. Mozambique is a country recovering from the ravages of civil war. Many women who have been left without husbands are struggling to bring up children on their own, their main income being from small-scale farming. In inhospitable terrain, they grow their maize and peanuts. Visitors from Britain who went to see how these women were managing were given a rapturous welcome, but, more significantly, a rapturous departure. To send them on their way the women formed a queue and each gave the visitors something from their fields to take away – a few ears of maize or a handful of peanuts. These women, some of the poorest in the world, wanted to share the little they had with some of the richest people. The widow's mite became a reality in the twenty-first century and gave a powerful message about the true meaning of sharing.

God the disturber, in this time of Lent, the season of giving and sacrifice, teach us the true meaning of sharing. Thank you for what we can learn from those who by worldly standards have little to give, but who by the standards of your kingdom are wealthy indeed.

Day 10

The greatest in the kingdom
Matthew 18:1–6

Unless you change and become like little children, you will never enter the kingdom of heaven. (Matthew 18:3)

What could possibly make a child greater than an adult? In worldly terms, probably very little, and in Jesus' time even less. Children had no status, their opinions were not sought, and they could not legally own property. In fact, historians tell us that children were no better than slaves.

We read very little in the Bible about children. Apart from his escapade at the Temple when he was twelve, we know virtually nothing about Jesus as a child. Children were not deemed to be people in their own right until they reached adulthood, so this makes it all the more remarkable that Jesus took a child as his example of greatness.

But Jesus reverses all the human ideas of greatness. The child in her dependent state – dependent on nurture and care from others – is the one to be emulated, not the people who can stand on their own, dependent neither on God nor on others. And not only were the disciples themselves to become humble, like children, but they had actively to welcome these children. The weakest among them were to be given respect. The rules of social conduct were to be changed and based on humility and service rather than on power and authority.

Imagine how radically our communities would be altered if the ground rules about power were changed so dramatically. What would it be like if we were all so dependent on each other in the way that children are dependent? What would it be like if children were given a voice and their opinions mattered? What would the life of our churches be like if worship and service focused on the needs of children?

And children can be great instruments of change. In South India, groups of children have been taught puppetry, drama and song and have been the messengers going round villages teaching about sanitation, domestic violence and bonded labour. Conventional wisdom would say that this is the realm of adult action, but the children have been remarkably effective. They were the ones who convinced their elders that new ideas were not all bad – after all, what harm can a toilet do to you!

Loving God, you could have walked this earth in splendour and might, but instead chose to come among us as a little child. Help us to learn that the world's view of greatness is not your way, and may we follow you in dependence and humility.

Day 11

All one in Christ
Galatians 3:23–8

There is neither Jew nor Greek, slave nor free, male nor female, for you are all one in Christ Jesus. (Galatians 3:28)

Every morning devout Jews would say their morning prayer of thanksgiving, which included thanking God that 'Thou has not made me a Gentile, a slave or a woman'. But in Christ, those barriers that previously existed are broken down. The old distinctions are removed and a new way of community has come into being. In this new life all the distinctions of race, caste and gender have been discarded. Instead of division, there is now equality.

This has dramatic implications for the way in which the New Testament Church and the Church today should conduct its social relations. For Jews, the law had regulated life, and it established, as we saw in Deuteronomy, that the poor and excluded were not to be taken advantage of. In this new life in Christ, we are no longer bound by the law because we should automatically want to ensure that life is fairer and that the weak are protected. If we are truly one, then we must want all our brothers and sisters to have life in all its fullness. If we want that and believe it, it must affect the way we relate to others.

A new barrier that is emerging in some parts of the world is HIV/AIDS. People who are HIV-positive are in many places stigmatised and ostracised and the Church has not always been the first to welcome them. Not so in Lilanda, on the outskirts of Lusaka. Lilanda is extremely poor, but there the love of God shines out like a beacon. Zambia has one of the world's highest incidences of AIDS. In Lilanda no one knows how many people are HIV-positive, but they do know that there are hundreds of orphans and dozens of sick and dying people. The women of the parish have, on a voluntary basis, become home carers. As far as they are able, they support all those in the parish who need care. No one is excluded. They are active in smashing the barriers, and building a parish that may be physically weak but is a spiritual giant.

Lord Jesus, you actively sought out people who were excluded – lepers, Samaritans and women. You welcomed them and spent time with them. Give us the vision, as your Church, to welcome those who are excluded, and to be people who break down barriers rather than those who build or perpetuate them.

Day 12

SECOND SUNDAY IN LENT:
'I AM THE GOOD SHEPHERD'

JOHN M. HULL

John 10:11–16

*The man runs away because he is a hired hand . . .
I am the good shepherd . . . I lay down my life
for the sheep. (John 10:13, 14, 15)*

In this passage we find a contrast between the person who is motivated merely by money and the one who has accepted real responsibility.

The hired man has a certain attitude to his job. He does it for the money, and we must agree that there is nothing wrong with that. Most of us are obliged by our economic system to work, but when you work for money there is a limit to what you are prepared to do. The hired man was happy to keep an eye on the sheep but fighting wolves was not in the contract!

The shepherd who owns the sheep has an altogether different attitude. He knows the name of each sheep. The good shepherd will defend the sheep against the wolves.

We live in a world dominated by money. Money enters almost every aspect of our lives – those who have money enjoy better health and tend to live longer. Children quickly learn that what adults want most is money. Is there any point in resisting this type of society? We must resist unless we want our human values to become the values of money. But how can we resist? Where can we find resources to empower such a resistance?

In the Christian faith we find a different set of values – the values of love, of solidarity with each other, of responsibility and of self-giving. In this tradition, strangers are welcome regardless of their financial position; and people cannot be reduced to monetary values because each person has a name and is individually cared for.

Christian faith, however, is not just a set of values, nor just a series of noble ideals. It is a dynamic reality centred upon the living God who in Jesus Christ made the values of love and freedom concrete, and demonstrated God's absolute commitment by the laying down of his life. It is because the action of God through Jesus Christ is still alive in the world that we can find courage and faith to resist the domination of money.

This passage calls upon us to look forward to a new society in which all barriers will come down and we will live in solidarity with each other.

Lord Jesus Christ, you are the good shepherd. Your sacrificial love is still at work in the world calling us to enter into the kind of life that you live. Open our hearts and set our imaginations free to follow you.

Day 13

WELCOMING THE STRANGER

GARTH HEWITT

Loving the stranger
Deuteronomy 10:12–22

The LORD your God . . . shows no partiality and accepts no bribes. He defends the cause of the fatherless and the widow, and loves the alien, giving him food and clothing. And you are to love those who are aliens, for you yourselves were aliens in Egypt. (Deuteronomy 10:17–19)

This passage reminds us of the character of God, and, because of this character, of what are the moral requirements for us. It is a moving passage that shows us that God is free of favouritism and cannot be bribed. He requires justice for orphans, widows and strangers. This is the God who cared for the vulnerable in a world where there were no social services, and so orphans and widows were particularly vulnerable – as were strangers who had no family to look after them.

During this week I will be thinking particularly of the Dalit community of India, where I have spent time with Dalit organisations in several different parts of the country. The Dalits were formerly called the 'untouchables' or 'outcastes'.

In one southern Indian village that I visited, a landlord had taken the common land and asked a Dalit administrator to cover up what he had done and make it look legal. This man, Chinnakanu, refused, and so the landlord bribed and threatened various people and Chinnakanu lost his job as a result. Repeatedly we came across situations where bribes were used and where the police force and the authorities were not impartial. It is good, therefore, to be reminded of the character of a God who shows no partiality and accepts no bribes, and it is this that lies behind the Dalits' pronouncement that, as Dalit theologian A. P. Nirmal puts it, Dalits considered as 'no people become God's people'.

God shows love of the stranger and calls for the community to love those who are strangers. For the people of Israel this was a reminder that they were once strangers in Egypt and, therefore, they must always be committed to the stranger in their midst. We too have a responsibility to care for the stranger, particularly for refugees and asylum seekers who come to our country, often in desperate need and having travelled through traumatic circumstances. As followers of this compassionate God, we are called to show the same values.

> God – the friend of the orphan, the widow and the stranger,
> God – with whom there is no prejudice or partiality – who
>   accepts no bribes,
> May we be part of a community that walks in your footsteps
>   and shows your justice and compassion to all.

Day 14

Healing the lepers
Matthew 8:1–4

A man with leprosy came and knelt before him and said,
'Lord, if you are willing, you can make me clean.'
Jesus reached out his hand and touched the man.
'I am willing,' he said. (Matthew 8:2–3)

In today's reading we find Jesus the healer who is not afraid to touch the leper or the person with a skin disease, even though the Levitical law describes them as unclean. To touch them was, therefore, to pollute oneself, but Jesus did not hesitate. So the kingdom of God arrives in action. Once again, the relevance of the gospel to today is seen poignantly. The Dalits of India are considered impure and untouchable. In Tsundur, in Andhra Pradesh, eight Dalits were massacred on 6 August 1991. The massacre was sparked off because Dalits sat in the same cinema seats as upper caste people and accidentally the foot of one of them touched an upper caste person. 'How dare your feet touch ours?' was the response and they attacked them and killed them in the fields near their village. To this day, the culprits have not been punished.

The message of the kingdom of God is that purity systems are challenged. Now no one is impure, no one is untouchable, no one an outcast. In Jewish tradition, the ability to heal lepers was felt to be a sign of the Messiah himself, though the Qumran community of the Essenes said that no one is allowed to meet the Messiah who 'is smitten in his flesh, paralysed in his feet and hands, or lame, or blind, or deaf, or dumb, or smitten in his flesh with a visible blemish'.

However, Jesus comes and says that the kingdom of God is 'good news for the poor', and brings in a community of new values based on the principles of Jubilee. The message that Jesus brings is to cast out the demons of exploitation, to touch where oppressive rules have said 'don't touch'.

This is liberation indeed – and what about within our own community? We all know that there are those who, in some sense of the word, are untouchable. Perhaps because they are asylum seekers. Maybe they are outcasts of the Church because of their sexual orientation. These are deep challenges to all of us because Jesus reached out and touched.

God who makes whole, may we be disciples of Jesus, learning well the lesson of the inclusive kingdom that welcomes and asserts the value of all. And in this wonderful liberation may we ourselves be refreshed to realise we are all acceptable in the love of God.

Day 15

*When Jesus saw him lying there and learned that he had
been in this condition for a long time, he asked him,
'Do you want to get well?' 'Sir, . . . I have no-one to help
me into the pool . . .' Then Jesus said to him, 'Get up!
Pick up your mat and walk.' (John 5:6–8)*

If you are in East Jerusalem it is fascinating to visit the ruins of
the Pool of Bethesda. The Pool is where this man found liberation from his disability through Jesus the healer. Jesus, who helps
and heals, is immediately criticised afterwards for healing on the
Sabbath. Strict religious people were shocked to see the sick man
carrying his mat as the law forbade it, and they asked him, 'Who
is this fellow who told you to pick it up and walk?' Jesus broke the
Sabbath, spoke of God as his father, and said, 'My father is always
at his work to this very day, and I, too, am working.' In John's
Gospel it is claimed that it was for this reason that the antagonism
mounted against Jesus that was eventually to lead to his death.

By law, the Dalits of India should not be oppressed, but in
practice they are held back and victimised in every way. At Tamil
Nadu Theological College, when asked for a favourite passage from
the Bible, one of the staff offered the one we have just read, and in
particular the words 'pick up your mat and walk'. They feel this is
what they are being asked to do. No one has helped them at the
pool, so to speak, so they are doing it for themselves. Dalit
Christians feel affirmed by Jesus and identify with him as the one
who walks beside them on this journey.

In one village in Tamil Nadu there is a Dalit woman who, during India's fiftieth anniversary of independence, was asked to raise the flag. However, a dominant upper caste member in the village had her beaten unconscious and she remains completely traumatised by the incident. This is the kind of abuse and victimisation so many people suffer. In some ways this woman is now a broken spirit; and what the Dalit theologians are trying to do is to restore the broken spirits and say to them, 'Get up! Pick up your mat and walk.'

Do we too affirm the forgotten in our midst and campaign for them around the world? Are we part of the liberated community or the limiting community?

> *God of all, it is so hard to live on the margins – lonely and*
>   *forgotten,*
> *despised . . . dependent . . . remember me, put back my confi-*
>   *dence*
> *Restore my dignity*
> *And walk down the edges with me . . .*
> *Then, knowing the Lord, I shall rise . . . rise in hope.*[1]

Day 16

Jews and Samaritans
John 4:7-15

The Samaritan woman said to him, 'You are a Jew and I am a Samaritan woman. How can you ask me for a drink?' (For Jews do not associate with Samaritans.) (John 4:9)

This extraordinary story shows the inclusiveness of Jesus' ministry, as he crosses all barriers to welcome strangers: barriers of sex, race and religion. First of all, he is talking to a woman – and the disciples' astonishment when they return to see him doing this is reflected later in verse 27. Also, Jesus is breaking the power of the Temple, saying that where you worship is not important. He is, furthermore, breaking racial and religious barriers. Samaritans were a kind of 'middle' race: Gentiles used to regard them as Jews, while the Jews saw them as foreigners. Not surprisingly, the Jews and Samaritans did not normally associate with one another.

A friend of mine, Rabbi Jeremy Milgrom, is like this. He is the co-ordinator for Rabbis for Human Rights, committed to justice and peace for both Palestinian and Jew. When Palestinian homes are being bulldozed by the Israeli army he goes and sits in front of the bulldozers to try and stop them. His closest friend is a Muslim who lives in a refugee camp in Bethlehem.

Among the Dalit community, drawing water from a well is a big issue. Upper caste people do not like them using the same well. Although sometimes special taps or cups are allocated, there is often conflict against Dalits at wells. It almost seems symbolic that water, which we all need for life, is a place of conflict.

Jesus says, '. . . a time is coming when you will worship the Father neither on this mountain nor in Jerusalem . . . a time is coming and has now come when the true worshippers will worship the Father in spirit and truth . . .' (John 4:21, 23). So it is not the location that is important. Perhaps we could add 'It is not the denomination', nor is it people from a special part of the world or membership of a certain group. True worship is worshipping in spirit and truth and, as Jesus shows by his actions, it is living out justice, respect and dignity for all. This is the way we, too, are called to live.

Jesus, you are the water of life: refresh us today. You are the way of life: strengthen us by your spirit to make you visible by our love in action. Yours is the gift of life: may we offer that same gift of love to the stranger in need.

Day 17

But who is my neighbour?
Luke 10:25–37

*'Which of these three do you think was a neighbour to
the man who fell into the hands of robbers?' The expert
in the law replied, 'The one who had mercy on him'.
Jesus told him, 'Go and do likewise.' (Luke 10:36–7)*

The new *Jerome Biblical Commentary* on this passage says, 'This famous example story . . . is meant to arrest the readers' attention and impel them to imitate the conduct of a pariah, a Samaritan.' Today, the word *pariah* is commonly used as an example of someone who is an outcast, but it actually originates in India and it is a reference to a group within the Dalits who had the responsibility for playing the drums on various significant occasions. The reason drums were given to outcastes to play was because they had to touch the skins of dead animals to make the drums, and to play them. The Dalits, therefore, can read this story as the parable of the Good Dalit. They understand exactly what Jesus is talking about – people who were considered unclean, or in some sense polluted, are welcomed into the kingdom of God.

Down the road from where I live in Stepney is Brick Lane and there is a fascinating building there that is a parable in itself. When the Huguenots fled to Britain as refugees from France they formed a community of weavers around the Spitalfields area, and they built a chapel. They were Protestants who had fled persecution on religious grounds. Later, this chapel was turned into a synagogue as Jewish refugees came to this part of the East End. Oswald

Moseley was to march against the Jews in Brick Lane with his Black Shirts. Now the building has turned into a mosque and members of the British Lone community originate predominantly from Bangladesh. Political extremists have attacked Brick Lane in relatively recent times, and only three years ago I saw a burnt-out house with racist slogans on it. What each of the groups that have used this bulding have in common is the experience of being refugees and strangers and the need to be welcomed. How can we turn the tide of negative thinking about refugees in our own community? Perhaps we have to rediscover the way of telling the parable of the Good Asylum Seeker, because ours is the God who calls strangers to come close and calls for a community that welcomes them.

May God's justice strengthen you,
the reconciliation of the Holy Spirit be in all your encounters
And the love of Christ live in you as you go out into the world.[2]

Day 18

When were you a stranger?
Matthew 25:31–40

I tell you the truth, whatever you did for one of the least of these brothers of mine, you did for me. (Matthew 25:40)

This familiar passage is deeply challenging and affirming of the most forgotten people in our world. When we reach out to those who are considered to be the least, we are reaching out to Jesus.

'Who are the least?' They are the most vulnerable or the most invisible. They may be child labourers. They may be street children who are used as prostitutes. They may be the Dalits, victimised and abused and still suffering under a feudal system. They may be, as the Anglican Bishop of Jerusalem, Bishop Riah Abu el Assal, says, the Palestinian Church that is invisible to the World Church. They may be those who are trapped in Third World debt, or in human rights abuse, or victims of an unjust trade system. Our kingdom values challenge us to live in a way that will make them visible and bring liberation. Can we hear them? Can we see them? Do we speak up for them? Have we prayed for them? Have we listened to them and learnt from them?

In India I met an old man called Tangevelu. He had a sparkle in his eye, and for years he had battled in the village for rights and for land for the Dalit community. He said, 'Two years ago I found a new faith': he had become a Christian and now had a Christian name – Daniel. His reasons were fascinating. It was, he said, because Christianity cares for others – it sees people as equal. It says do good to others. No one is ruled out. As I listened to

Tangevelu, I wondered whether we actually live up to the principles that he was describing. What he had seen in Christianity was absolutely right and is what Jesus outlines in this passage – but too often Christians have espoused class or caste, racial prejudice or status. We can carry out these words of Jesus by welcoming the stranger; by rejecting preferential treatment for the wealthy, the powerful and the upper class. The way of Jesus is commitment to the most vulnerable, and justice for all.

> *Compassionate God, on this week's journey we have seen you reaching out to the weak, and challenging us to be a community that welcomes the stranger. In the words and example of Jesus we are called to love in a costly way, to go against the values of our world. May we be faithful to this vision.*

Day 19

THIRD SUNDAY IN LENT:
'I AM THE TRUE VINE'

INDERSIT BHOGAL

John 15:1–17

---

*If you obey my commands, you will
remain in my love. (John 15:10)*

Now remain in my love. (John 15:9)

John's Gospel is often seen to present an otherworldly Jesus who
has no relevance to the struggles and sufferings of people in
daily life experiences. But here we see that the Gospel offers
interpretations of Jesus that emerge from real experiences of people;
experiences of persecution by, and exclusion from, the dominant
community.

John 15:1–17 should be read after John 15:18–25 and John
16:2. As Johannine Christians struggle with those who exercise
power and control over them, they are reminded that they are
sustained by following Jesus: 'If you obey my commands, you will
remain in my love' and so 'abide with me' (NRSV). And previously
they have been reminded that participating in Holy Communion
is a way of abiding in Christ (John 6:56).

The Johannine Christian community is warned of hatred and
persecution as they engage with the ruling authorities. They find
strength and encouragement in remembering that this was Jesus'
experience too (John 15:20 and 16:33). The bond between Jesus
and his followers is thus strengthened, and they 'abide' in him.

John's Gospel has relevance for people who face persecution and oppression. People who suffer and struggle as they challenge injustice can interpret their own experiences in the light of Jesus' experience, just as the Johannine Christian community did.

Christians facing hardship and struggle throughout the world can interpret and give some meaning to their experience in the light of Jesus' experience. Christians in 'Third World' countries have done this creatively and thus found a way of abiding, and finding strength, in Jesus. Christian asylum seekers who find themselves imprisoned in Britain shouted loud amens when I shared this with them on visits to Detention Centres. They find encouragement, hope and sustenance in worship. They abide in Jesus through a continuing loyalty to him, through prayer and by sharing in Holy Communion.

Prison life is lonely and isolates a person. The opportunity to pray and eat with others is a healing experience. Such communion strengthens them as they challenge authorities and seek justice for themselves.

Holy God
Thank you for the honour you give us by creating us in your
  own image,
and for showing us in Jesus that you abide with us at all times
  and in all places.
Forgive us
for all the ways in which we betray our faith.
We bless you
for the memory of Jesus Christ.
Unite us with him in our daily life and through our
  communion at your table,
that we may remain in you, and you in us.

Day 20

CHALLENGING THE POWERS

DAVID PAIN

The cost of discipleship
Matthew 8:18–22

Another disciple said to him, 'Lord, first let me go and bury my father.' But Jesus told him, 'Follow me, and let the dead bury their own dead.' (Matthew 8:21–2)

What could be more important than burying a parent? Jesus challenges a responsibility that goes to the heart of relationships that exist within families. This must have been as shocking to the Gospel writers as it is to us today. What kind of discipleship is it that challenges this family duty?

During this week we reflect on the implications of Jesus' life, death and resurrection for our relationship with the powers. The biblical use of 'principalities and powers' comes from a particular worldview; although our view of the world has changed since biblical times, many Christians continue to find challenge and inspiration from Jesus' approach to the powers. They are the structures, systems, traditions and assumptions that guide and govern our politics, economy and society. They can work for the good of us all, or can be misdirected to the benefit of the few. The powers were created through Christ, and therefore in and through Jesus there is hope for their transformation.

The powers that govern social, political and economic organisation do not just exist outside us. As we discern the nature of these forces we are increasingly aware of their presence and influence within our own lives and spirituality, for our nature is influenced by the spirit of our times. So what does this passage say about Jesus challenging such forces? What kind of family values do we find in the reign of God?

These powers can be experienced as working for or against the reign of God. We learn ways of relating to each other from inherited tradition, experience and the media. These can lead us to seek to dominate, abuse or exploit other people. But Jesus, who washes his disciples' feet, demonstrates that relationships in the reign of God, including family ones, are based on service. Jesus challenges the relationships and institutions by which we live. Unlike even the animals, he himself has 'no place to lay his head'. Jesus' mission is an urgent one, and his disciples must acknowledge that. His words here are a telling reminder that all forms of social organisation, including families, are secondary to the will of God.

I bring before you all the relationships of which I am part, the experiences of joy and pain that they involve. The message of your reign shocks and challenges me and I offer those feelings to you too. I pray that you will transform the relationships that govern my family, community and nation.

Day 21

The challenge of discipleship
Matthew 10:16–23

Brother will betray brother to death, and a father his child; children will rebel against their parents and have them put to death. (Matthew 10:21)

This verse brings to mind images from Rwanda. In 1994, in the space of 100 days, nearly a million people were hacked to death, many by neighbours. Family members were betrayed by one another and handed over to the death squads. In his reflection on Rwanda, Fergal Keane writes that the killers were 'not born to hate, but learned to hate'. Hatred and division were endemic over many generations and, in the run-up to the killing, fears and divisions were systematically promoted and exploited by those with power. Keane also challenges us in asking 'what kind of man' can be involved in such killing, and concludes that any one of us has that potential: we can all be manipulated by the powers of division and hatred.

The powers are often experienced as working against the reign of God, in the suffering they create in violence, poverty, racism, greed, pollution and despotism. How can we challenge such destructive power?

In our discipleship we are invited to join a process of challenging the powers, and as we do so we cannot expect a false peace where none exists; instead, we must enter the reality of suffering and conflict. Mark 13 portrays the coming reign of God like a gathering storm; conflict and division seem endemic. The parables suggest that the coming reign of God is not about incremental change, as the reformers have suggested; nor is it about a revolution that simply replaces one oppressive system with another. Rather, it is like yeast working within a dough, slowly but powerfully rising, bringing about a total transformation from within.

In Rwanda the legacy of genocide and trauma remains, yet people today are working to build a new future out of this tragedy.

In each generation prophets have discerned the reign of God challenging the life-denying powers. As we reflect on the world around us, how might our discipleship lead us to challenge the powers, which are counter to the reign of God? How can we seek ways in which the powers will be transformed to become life-giving?

Violence and hatred are all around me, and most of all within me. Open my eyes to the wonderful possibilities for justice, healing and peace that your reign offers. I take strength from those who embrace the legacy of division and fear in their daily lives, and I seek all that is life-affirming through the power of your spirit.

Day 22

*Because of my chains, most of the brothers and sisters
in the Lord have been encouraged to speak the word
of God more courageously and fearlessly.
(Philippians 1:14, NIV Inclusive)*

In what ways does the witness of others strengthen us to challenge the powers? Paul's witness to Jesus brings him into conflict with the Roman authorities. Paul is taken prisoner by the powers and yet his imprisonment serves the purpose of the gospel.

Before Constantine converted the Roman Empire to Christianity, Christians expected to live against the culture and values of their time. Since Constantine, in many countries Christianity has been closely associated with the ruling system, the preservation of which has been seen as integrally linked to Christian living.

The witness of many people against the apartheid system in South Africa brought them into conflict with a system that claimed that apartheid was the will of God; exposing this heresy led to persecution and cost many their liberty. Many defied apartheid in daily acts of non-co-operation with the system. Others went to prison for their beliefs. The most famous prisoners were held on Robben Island, and among them was Nelson Mandela. The campaign against apartheid became synonymous with the campaign for his release.

Visiting the island prison, tourists are guided around by former inmates who speak both of the hardship of imprisonment – but also of how they took strength from it. Those who spent many years locked up as political prisoners learnt much from each other, and their moral strength on release is unparalleled. Even more striking, however, are the stories of the prison guards who found inspiration from prisoners who the system told them were evil and dangerous.

Apartheid is over, but new challenges are faced in that country – not least the HIV/AIDS pandemic and structural poverty to which it is closely linked. Recovering from the impact of the powers of oppression locally and internationally will not happen quickly.

Jesus died the death of a criminal and a political prisoner, an experience of suffering that many persecuted Christians have had to share. This suffering is integral to the role Jesus has in challenging the authority of the powers. The testimony of Paul and other prisoners of conscience encourages and surprises us in our mission to challenge the powers.

> *I take courage from other people who have struggled against the powers. Thank you for the inspiration of those who have gone before and those I journey with now. As I remember people important to me, may I draw energy from their lives and their defiance of the powers.*

Day 23

Paul and the king
Acts 26:19–26

*The Christ would suffer and, as the first to rise
from the dead, would proclaim light to his
own people and to the Gentiles. (Acts 26:23)*

Paul's testimony to King Agrippa tells of the inevitability of suffering for Jesus, and his own experience on the road to Damascus had convinced him of the centrality of this message.

The life and ministry of Jesus was a systematic challenge to the powers of the religious authorities. Jesus breaks through the boundaries defined by the holiness laws, meeting and eating with those who are considered unclean, 'sinners'. The powers have put in place rules that exclude and marginalise; by contrast, the reign of God is a hope for life that crosses all the previous barriers, bringing 'light both to our people and to the Gentiles'.

In our day, those who work with people living with leprosy or with HIV infection continue to expose such prejudices. People living with leprosy in India have been thrown out of their homes and villages; the witness of Christian religious and medical staff has been a profound witness to the truth that the Christian gospel challenges such boundaries of exclusion.

Jesus presents a clear and present danger to the authority of those who have a vested interest in the status quo. The religious authorities have no option but to hand him over for execution by the Romans.

The cross is the ultimate sanction of the powers; they can do no more than this to a man who dares to challenge their authority.

It is in the cross that the powers are exposed, and instead of this being their moment of victory it is the beginning of their defeat. Colossians 2:15 tells us that the cross unmasks the powers, reveals the limitations of their authority.

The world-changing experience of the followers of Jesus is that his death is not an end, and this is deeply threatening to the powers. Paul tells Agrippa that 'for this reason the Jews seized me in the temple and tried to kill me'.

The politics of hope is the politics of the cross. This means not avoiding the cost of challenging the powers, but embracing it freely – dying to the authority of the powers and transforming them in the process.

Meeting you takes me one step further in the inevitable progress of your reign. As I shed the barriers created by the powers, their weight lifts and the journey moves on. Each step may be hesitant, but as I respond to your invitation I know there can be no other way.

Day 24

The Church under pressure
Revelation 3:7–13

*Let anyone who has an ear listen to what the Spirit
is saying to the churches. (Revelation 3:13, NRSV)*

John writes against the background of the Christian community
faced with the power of the Roman Empire. As a metaphor,
this has been read as the unfolding story of the struggle between
the living God and the powers of evil. The powers have sought to
take to themselves the authority that is of God alone. In such a
context, what is the Spirit saying to the churches?

We need to discern the places (whether at home and with our
family, on our televisions, in our community, supermarket, work-
place or nation) where the powers have become idolatrous. Rather
than acknowledging their createdness and therefore responsibility
to God, they have come to exist for their own purposes, not for
the greater good of humanity.

How do we then challenge the powers? The defeat of the powers
comes from dying to their control, both in the way in which society
is organised and within ourselves. As we expose the myth by which
the powers retain their hold over us and die to their influence over
us, we can acknowledge God to be the centre of our lives, the light
within.

Political engagement with the powers in the Jubilee 2000
movement and in campaigns to change the rules of trade can be
spiritually draining for campaigners. This leads many back to
explore their faith and draw upon the well of their shared spirituality. We can feel overwhelmed, but the following verse offers us

reassurance – 'I know that you have little strength, yet you have kept my word and have not denied my name' (Revelation 3:8b).

We cannot force change; our witness is to recognise the light of God within everyone, and to invite others to respond. This invitation is not a weak hope, but a confident belief. Our hope is sure because, as we read in this passage, 'See, I have placed before you an open door that no-one can shut' (Revelation 3:8a). We can be confident in our ability to challenge the powers because our confidence is in the things God is able to do, not in saving us from the world and the powers, but in transforming them and us.

Open my ears to hear the word of the Spirit. My experience of the Christian community brings assurance of your life-giving ways. As I challenge the influence of the powers I seek to renew my energy, drawing ever deeper on you, the light within, today and always.

Day 25

Commissioned and empowered
Luke 24:44–9

The Christ will suffer and rise from the dead on the third day, and repentance and forgiveness of sins will be preached in his name to all nations . . . you are witnesses of these things. (Luke 24:46–8)

We have seen this week how the life, death and resurrection of Jesus is a source of hope for our lives as we live within our social, economic and political system. What is the nature of our commission to witness to these things?

In Jesus we find a model for challenging the powers. Jesus was executed because the way he lived challenged authority. His resurrection assures us of the power of the reign of God in overcoming the death-dealing ways of the powers. This is not offered to us as a high ideal that cannot be attained, but as a lived reality. As disciples we are called to take the mission of Jesus to the world (John 20:21); as we stay rooted in Jesus, ours will be a politics of hope.

As witnesses to these things we are part of the process of the coming of God's reign; we are not spectators but actors; we are subjects, not objects, of history. The politics of hope by which we live is believing and living the future into being. Whenever we act on the basis of justice and trust, rather than out of fear and the need to dominate, we take the first step in making these hopes into a reality.

In our experience of living this future we can expect to have to wrestle with God, for the spirit of the coming reign is not yet fully formed. We struggle against what we are told is impossible. We struggle against everything within us that denies that we can change the world. The open door invites us to believe there can be another way. We denounce the myth that 'There Is No Alternative'.

The kingdom is about the reality of the world as we live in the grip of the powers. But it is also about the reality of God: Jesus who suffers and who meets us at the depth of despair about the world; Jesus who conquers the forces of death and lives on in the mission of his followers, in the midst of our broken reality.

I give thanks for the inspiration of the life, death and resurrection of Jesus, which gives me hope for life. I want to be part of the process of change; I believe that there is an alternative and I commit myself to living it into being, through the power of your Spirit.

Day 26

FOURTH SUNDAY IN LENT: 'I AM THE BREAD OF LIFE'

INDERJIT BHOGAL

John 6:25–40

You are looking for me, not because you saw miraculous signs but because you ate the loaves and had your fill. Do not work for food that spoils, but for food that endures to eternal life. (John 6:26–7)

We might expect Jesus to be frustrated that his words and actions continue to be misunderstood, and people fail to distinguish between 'food that spoils' and 'food that endures for eternal life'. However, the discussion here shows his deep patience and an attitude of forgiveness of people's failures. Having eaten with them, Jesus continues to nourish them.

Jesus connects with people through eating with them. Communing thus with him is also to feed on him. It is to be forgiven; to be fed and sustained by Jesus. In giving of himself in this way, Jesus gives life. In John, Jesus' followers, who failed, misunderstood and betrayed him again and again, find sustenance in the memory of the meals Jesus shared with them. And participating in Holy Communion sustains us in the context of daily life and struggles.

One of the most memorable meals I have had was given to me by Maria who lives on the slopes of a volcano in El Salvador. Maria gathers coffee beans left or dropped by coffee pickers. She sells them, keeping some back for herself. When I visited her, without prior arrangement, I was treated like an honoured guest.

She went out and collected wood, lit it, and placed a pan of water on it. Then she went out again and came back with a parcel. It was locally collected honey.

The water came to the boil. In went two large pinches of her own coffee. She gave me coffee and she gave me a small bowl of honey. She gave me what she could. When I left she gave me a little bag of coffee. About four tablespoons full. She bid farewell and said, 'Remember me.' I still have the coffee. I cannot bring myself to use it. It is too precious. It reminds me of her. I remember Maria whenever I have coffee or honey.

Bit by bit, poverty has consumed Maria's body. The honey and coffee she gave me was a sacramental meal. Its memory, kept alive by the coffee she gave me to bring home, continues to inspire and feed me.

> Holy God,
> we have tried so many ways to find you.
> Forgive us,
> for our failure to see you beside us,
> and communing with us.
> We bless you
> for staying with us,
> forgiving us, and feeding us
> in Jesus the Bread of Life,
> day by day.

Day 27

PEOPLE OF THE FUTURE

REBECCA DUDLEY

Asking forgiveness
Luke 7:36–50

Her many sins have been forgiven –
for she loved much. (Luke 7:47)

The woman who shocks a dinner party is not named (see Mark 14:3–9; Matthew 26:6–13). Her anonymity is a reminder of her status: she doesn't really count. She is a woman who enters a company of men. She is literally a woman of 'low repute' – though maybe not a prostitute – entering a company of respected public figures in the community. She is a sinner. They are professionally pious. She lowers herself to the level of their feet, while they talk face to face. They continued to debate and argue as intellectual friends might. She touches Jesus.

But there is more. She carries a fragrant perfume into the middle of the room that mingles with the smells from the 'kitchen' area in which other women must have been at work. The other women in this story (surely Simon didn't do his own cooking?) are invisible; she is front and centre in the story. Her emotions – tears of brokenness – soft and vulnerable, contrast with the 'hard' welcome she receives from the hosts of the house. Finally, as Jesus notices (vv. 44 ff) – in contrast to Simon's mean welcome – her tears and hair combined with the expensive ointment, for which she would have paid some days' wages, to form a gift of herself. The sensuality of touch, fragrance and passion must have been, to say the least, embarrassing.

In fact, given the power of her actions, it is extraordinary that she has no speaking part at all in this drama. The source of the power is her faith and love.

Jesus is the bridge to bring women back into the community at a higher level of dignity than before. But woman herself has initiated the action, with humility that came from faith, and confidence born out of love. Martin Luther King, the US civil rights leader, captured the astonishing power of this action in his own words: 'Everybody can be great. Because anybody can serve. You only need a heart full of grace, and a soul generated by love.' Here, purposeful, determined love re-establishes a relationship with God.

Lord, there are times I have felt estranged from you. But now I want to know your saving presence, your loving gaze. I need your help to do better, and to live at peace with you and others.

Day 28

Forgiving others
Matthew 18:21–35

. . . unless you forgive your brother from your heart.
(Matthew 18:35)

'Forgiveness is a process by which people are freed from a bondage that locks them to some past evil.'[3] Non-payment of debts used to be a crime for which you could be locked up and – more importantly for the purposes of Jesus' teaching – ultimately released. The point of forgiveness is release.

Here Jesus' teaching is directed at the victim, the one who has something to forgive. Jesus argues that the victims are also sinners, who extend forgiveness because it has been extended to them. This seems all right in the cases where the sinner repents, makes amends and changes. Forgiveness is granted to release new possibilities.

Peter asks how many times he must forgive, and Jesus gives an extraordinary answer: seventy-seven times. A reminder, and reversal, of the violent intentions expressed by the descendant of Cain, Lamech. He describes his retaliatory code: 'If Cain is avenged seven times, then Lamech seventy-seven times' (Genesis 4:24). It is a culture all too contemporary among street gangs in countless cities, and in civil conflicts that have continued for generations: tragic cycles in which violence – sins – will continue to mount and make an untold impact on families and societies. Jesus is acknowledging a tradition that has been developed to deal with serious violence, not just minor infractions and discourtesies.

Seen from the point of view of the victims, forgiveness raises some disturbing questions – for example, in countries that have seen genocide, or for people who have been abused: '[For some,] forgiveness is the only option, indeed is the only way of remaining sane. Some say that reconciliation has to be first with God, and only then can it be with the neighbour. Or is it rather that the God to whom we must be reconciled is the one who comes to us in the person of our neighbour, even the neighbour who has committed the greatest crimes against us?'[4] For some, linking peace with God and neighbour so profoundly becomes a path to release from the past, to start building the future in their country. They choose that disturbing, difficult path to freedom.

> God, where the cycle of violence seems deep and intractable, strengthen those whose deepest desire is for release. Show them the way out.

Day 29

Forgiveness from the cross
Hebrews 10:11–18

By one sacrifice he has made perfect for ever those who are being made holy. (Hebrews 10:14)

In the ancient Jewish law, a sacrifice had to be repeated each time the relationship with God was broken. Leviticus 16:20 describes the 'scapegoat' ritual in which the sins of the people would be symbolically transferred to an animal, who would then 'carry on itself all their sins to a solitary place'. The writer of Hebrews wants to emphasise that Jesus' death was the final and decisive sacrifice for all time. But there was more: Jesus was not only the sacrifice, but also the priest. Jesus is a victim who takes all the sin of the world upon himself, much as the goat did. But he is also God who can grant forgiveness for all who accept and believe in the sacrifice of himself.

People who work for a community – ministers, teachers, social workers – can sometimes absorb into themselves all the community's problems. In Tower Hamlets, working in the community means confronting politics that sometimes feel corrupt, racist violence, poverty, crime, high rates of substance abuse, and the consequences of years of despair and neglect. And there are psychological problems. Newspapers, family members, and even colleagues from outside the area sometimes give the impression that they think community people – neighbours – are worthless scroungers if they are asylum seekers, or just poor. These are the kinds of sins that go beyond one person. They depress the spirit and batter you psychologically. But here is the good news of this text: Jesus has offered to take these community sins on himself. In our minds and hearts, we can 'hand over' the burden of them.

This is what I believe theologians mean when they assert that forgiveness from the cross never replaces justice, but instead goes beyond it. We don't have to carry the sins of whole communities and nations, like the scapegoats in Leviticus, into the wilderness of despair and hopelessness. God invites us to acknowledge them, and hand them over. And that handing over can free us up to serve more lightly, more joyfully, knowing that God expects us to do one person's work, with the gifts he gives to do it.

I acknowledge the sins at work in this community and this country; bigger than any one person — prejudice, racism, poverty, neglect, lack of vision, despair, and others . . . [name these]. In my mind and heart, I hand them over to you. Let me walk lighter now.

Day 30

Marks of a forgiven disciple
John 21:15–19

Yes Lord, you know I love you. (John 21:15)

Contrast this intimate, passionate exchange with the conversations that reflect our own culture more closely (e.g. 'You are the weakest link: goodbye'). Peter is not going to be the weakest link in this new community of forgiven disciples, but one of the strongest. Jesus pointed him to the future, told him what to do, and expressed confidence in him. None the less, there is an element of sternness in the demands that Jesus puts on Peter. It is a hard role that Peter is given, particularly when readers later learn, in the tradition of the Church, that Peter follows his Lord so well that he is crucified in Rome under Nero (about 64 CE).

Jesus asks Peter three times if the disciple loves him; each time to recall the denials on the terrible night when the Lord was arrested: Peter, do you love me? Here, Christianity is reduced, or perhaps enlarged, to a relationship between the forgiven disciple and his Lord. Oscar Romero, the bishop from El Salvador who found his own martyrdom during that country's civil war in 1980, summarised the call to risky discipleship: 'Christianity is a person,' he wrote, 'one who loved us so much, and calls for our love. Christianity is Christ.'

There is something succinct and unavoidable in Jesus' demands on Peter. Michel Quoist, devotional writer, puts it this way:

Tomorrow God isn't going to ask,
What did you dream?

What did you think?
What did you plan?
What did you preach?
He is going to ask, 'What did you do?'

Or, to put it another way, after 40 years of campaigning by Amnesty International, it is not the letters we *meant* to write that released prisoners or got them better conditions. It is the ones that we actually *do* write.

But what exactly is Peter meant to do? His task is to be a leader of the Church, to nourish the ones who have been left leaderless. As a flawed, forgiven person, he becomes a magnificent leader of the Church. His task is to be the first to follow (vv. 18, 19).

> *With Peter and all your saints, in all the company of heaven and earth I pray: 'O Lord, forgive what I have been, sanctify what I am, and order what I shall be.'*[5]

Day 31

Marks of the forgiven community
Colossians 3:12–17

And over all these virtues put on love, which binds them all together in perfect unity. (Colossians 3:14)

Living in repentence means awareness of the common good. This is what the community looks like after it has 'put on the new self, which is being renewed in knowledge in the image of its Creator' (Colossians 3:10). The virtues here are not achievements, but attitudes: compassion, kindness, humility, gentleness and patience. Visible signs of the new life in community will be peace, unity, gratitude, openness to teaching and learning from each other, and – most of all – joy.

If we are honest, we must confess that this picture does not resemble any Christian community we know. The Church has failed on numerous occasions to live up to this ideal. If we are meant to 'put on love', what are the demands of love in the real world of failure and strife? Peter West of Christian Aid, visiting Rwanda in 2000, wrote: 'The failure of the church in Rwanda was not so much that some church leaders and pastors took part in the genocide, shocking though that may be, but that in the years when the conditions for the genocide were being built up, the church did not challenge what was happening . . . Is it that church-people often fail, not because we are "bad Christians", but because we do not understand the society we live in, and because Christian education hardly ever takes seriously our need to do so?'[6]

The story of Rwanda throws the challenge into stark relief: if we are serious about compassion, love and particularly about living at peace, we will confront the causes of strife and injustice before people are allowed to kill each other with impunity. The vision in Colossians keeps pulling us up to a new standard, to practise in the moment of history in which we find ourselves. As Ken Leech puts it: 'For his followers Jesus is the exact opposite of Humpty Dumpty. Not only is his broken life put together again in the resurrection, but each celebration of the Christian community is a . . . putting together of the Christ who was broken and smashed.'[7] That is part of the invitation, the need for continual renewal, in history, to be part of Christ.

By your grace, let me live as a forgiven person, in a forgiven community. Help me to practise compassion, kindness, humility and patience. Let others see the love that binds together the Christian community in which I am part of the living Christ.

Day 32

A world at peace
Micah 4:1–4

Every man will sit under his own vine and under his own fig-tree, and no-one will make them afraid. (Micah 4:4)

Here, actions of repentance and forgiveness shape international well-being, of individuals and nations. The world is restored to a right relationship with God. Weapons are turned into agricultural tools, so that people flourish instead of killing each other. In the same spirit, early twentieth-century advocates of childcare for women in London's East End converted a pub into a childcare facility. They changed the name from 'The Gunmaker's Arms' to 'The Mother's Arms'. But the vision in the Hebrew Scriptures equally evokes the pain, alienation and violence of a world at war with itself and with God (the pub was soon reacquired and the name changed back!).

After an 'aerial' view, the text zooms in on what peace means for individuals: a sufficient means of having wine and good things like figs, sufficient time to sit in the shade, freedom from anxiety and fear – what today we might call 'well-being'. The absence of external civil upheavals is closely connected to an absence of inner turmoil.

Researchers for the World Bank explored with people what they meant by 'well-being'. Their answers echoed the vision of the prophet. For women in Tabe Ere in rural Ghana, 'well-being means security: being protected by God, having children to give you security in old age, having a peaceful mind (*tiera villa*), patience (*kanyir*, meaning not holding a grudge against anyone), and plenty of rain'. Anxieties that threaten peace have to do with want as well as strife. Notice that the contented man beneath the fig-tree is not afraid of strife or hunger. As poor Bolivians have said, people who live 'well' are 'those who are not worried every day about what they are going to do tomorrow to get food for their children'.[8]

But as one Nicaraguan woman said in the midst of her country's civil war in the 1980s: 'You don't make peace by declaring it.'[9] The mountain of the Lord is the result of repentance, people turning their priorities around, as individuals and nations. In the words of the theologian Kosuke Koyama, 'The future belongs to those who repent.'

Help me to be a person of the future. I want to go beyond lamenting violence to repent of the things that make for violence. I want to go beyond declaring peace to making peace. May we walk your paths – in a community as wide as the world we share.

Day 33

FIFTH SUNDAY IN LENT: 'I AM THE WAY AND THE TRUTH AND THE LIFE'

LESLIE GRIFFITHS

John 14:1–11

Thomas said to him, 'Lord, we don't know where you are going, so how can we know the way?'
Jesus answered, 'I am the way and the truth and the life'. (John 14:5–6)

The second sermon I ever preached was on this text. It split itself up nicely into three sections, a gift for any preacher. Nowadays I wonder how I dared offer any thoughts about a verse that has gone on challenging me and goading me for all the forty years I've been preaching. It's still yielding its light and insight. I'm still struggling to get my mind round its huge claims.

Jesus said he was 'the way'. I was once driving through Haiti at a time of crisis. There were many police checkpoints where we needed to subject ourselves to inspection. I was so deep in conversation with a colleague that I drove straight through one such emplacement, the most notorious along the whole route. Within seconds I was being fired at by automatic weapons. I screeched to a halt, grovelled madly, answered the questions being put to me. 'Where are you coming from?' they thundered. 'And where are you headed?' Then, one last probe, 'How many passengers are you carrying?' A road is a road, a way is a way, when it takes people from a point of departure to a recognisable destination. Jesus claimed to be just that, to provide a pathway from where we are to where he wants us to go. That is the way of the cross and he invites us to tread it.

His claim to be the truth is equally daring. We've become accustomed to 'Truth and Reconciliation' commissions that attempt to put whole societies back together after long periods of division and strife. Only by owning one's past can one face one's future. Truth, said by Chairman Mao to come out of the barrel of a gun, actually comes from the deepest level of one's being. And Jesus, whose 'authority' was constantly commented upon, seems the very embodiment of such truth. His truth is not merely propositional but incarnational; he fleshes out the precepts he considers important. And it's life that he offers, life in all its fullness, a life on earth that's charged with the colours of heaven.

> Show us the way, dear Lord, your way, the way of self-sacrificing love, and reveal to us how, for all its pain and hardship, it leads to heaven.
>
> Bathe us in your truth, dear God, so that our lives may be stamped with the integrity we see in Jesus.
>
> And fan alive from within our deepest being, dear Lord, the flame of that faith which is life itself.

Day 34

REST FOR THE HEAVY LADEN

JANET WOOTTON

Water out of rock
Exodus 17:1–7

Strike the rock, and water will come out of it
for the people to drink (Exodus 17:6)

W ater is one of the most basic of human needs, and thirst one of the most devastating sensations. Without water, you would die in a few days, a horrible death. And yet millions of people live with the daily reality of thirst because they have no access, or difficult access, to clean drinking water.

Of course the people complained against Moses! They were in real danger. The parched land and hot air were sapping their very life. The miracle of water from the rock is very significant. For one thing, it was the rock of the desert, the dry land, which flowed with drinkable water. Refreshment flowed from the desert itself.

Then, the rod with which Moses struck the rock was the same one that stopped the water flowing at the Red Sea. Water is a necessity, but can also be a barrier. Floods kill and bring disease. While aboriginal Australians use their traditional skills to survive the harsh desert, the island communities in the Pacific face utter destruction through rising sea levels, in a bizarre pattern that is repeated around the globe.

To give life, sometimes communities need to provide water, but sometimes they need to protect against its ravages.

Jesus talks of the gift of God as the water of life or living water

(John 4:10–15; 7:37–9), which springs up from the heart of human life, banishing thirst for ever. It is clear in both places that he is not talking literally. There will still be a need to meet people's physical thirst. However, by using the image of water and the word 'thirst', Jesus shows how basic is people's longing for God.

Whether it is physical thirst or a longing for God, the letter to the Hebrews shows that complaining on its own will not do. The place where the Israelites complained was called 'Meribah', or 'complaining'. Hebrews 3:7–19 warns that stubbornness and complaining prevents people from entering rest – that is, from finding God.

The way forward is to bring the matter to God in prayer, to take action and find or offer refreshment, renewal and hope.

God, giver of living water, keep us from fruitless complaining against each other. Teach us to hear the cry of thirsty people and to work with all humankind to provide water to drink and wash in and enjoy. God, giver of living water, open our hearts to renewal and hope.

Day 35

Bread to spare
Luke 9:12–17

They all ate and were satisfied. (Luke 9:17)

Union Chapel Islington, like many other churches, runs a day centre for people who are homeless or badly housed. Although we offer services like showers, clothing and resettlement advice, the session centres on a copious hot meal.

Before the centre opens, a sullen queue builds up at the gate. There's lots of effing and blinding, pushing and shoving. Inside, the cook and volunteers are sweating away. Will there be enough meat? Why doesn't so and so help instead of sitting around? Tension builds.

Then the doors open and the people pour in. The tension explodes into festivity (on a good day). The distinction between 'users' and volunteers melts away in a riot of loudness and colour. There is *plenty* of food for everyone. Trouble starts when the eating is over, or when the latecomers find that they are too late to get a meal. That's when insults and, occasionally, fists fly.

People come not just because they are hungry, but because eating together creates an atmosphere of festivity. Many could eat in their isolated, grotty accommodation. But we share the need for company, for conversation and conviviality. A meal joins volunteers and guests, eaters and servers, in a festival of pleasure.

Jesus' words and actions release the same bounty. The hungry people are fed, in groups of about fifty, where they can sit and eat and talk: 'Did you see what he did?' 'Where did all this food come from?' 'Did you know that he healed my uncle's withered arm?'

'I've never heard teaching like that before.'

Jesus took the bread and fish, gave thanks to God, and broke up and distributed the food – words and actions of great power. These were the words and actions that characterised his last meal with his disciples and by which they recognised him after the resurrection (Luke 24:30–5). On each occasion, the actions of Jesus call for a response: to repeat the shared meal in his memory; to go and tell the others that Jesus is alive; and, here, to take the food round till everyone is fed.

> *Living Jesus, by your word of power and actions of love, call us to be your disciples. Remind us constantly of your love for all people. Send us out in your name to tell people that you are alive, and to make sure that, in this rich and fertile world, everyone has access to the food they need.*

Day 36

When there is no rest
Judges 19:26–30

[She] lay ... fallen in the doorway of the house,
with her hands on the threshold. (Judges 19:27)

This woman was a guest in the house of a stranger, she and her master. When the townspeople came howling for someone to abuse, she was the one with no protection. Her master let her go; the host did not refuse. She was sent out into the dark, into the arms of the mob, who raped her to death.

Her posture in death was one of seeking rest, trying to get home to safety, reaching out for a sanctuary that was not there.

The Bible is unremittingly realistic about the horrors that human beings can inflict on one another. The concubine dies; Tamar's life is destroyed by incest; David plots Uriah's death so that he can have access to Bathsheba. Households are disrupted and destroyed. Often, individual hurt spills into tribal bloodshed. The concubine's death results in the near destruction of one of the twelve tribes, saved only by the mass abduction of the other tribes' women.

Peoples are destroyed or driven into exile. Poverty deprives people of justice or even a place to lay their heads. Anyone who tries to sentimentalise or hide human suffering hears Jeremiah's condemnation on false prophets who say, 'Peace, peace', when there is no peace.

Even Jesus recognised that his good news would bring conflict. 'I do not come to bring peace', he said, 'but a sword ... Fathers will be against their sons ... mothers will be against their daughters' (Matthew 10:34–6).

And yet, peace, shalom, remains the great gift of God to his people. The kind of community in which people have access to the basic essentials of life, so that they have time to flourish, time to develop in love and friendship, time to shape their own lives, to learn and to achieve. This is what Jesus offers, life in all its fullness.

In this kind of community, children wouldn't be used for forced labour or prostitution, women would not fear violence in their own homes, men would never be driven out into the fields and shot into mass graves. All the hands that reached out for sanctuary would find it.

God, forgive us for all that abuses, blights and destroys human life. Heal the hurt in us, and reconcile us with each other. Help us to build communities that live at peace, where all people have the right to life in all its fullness.

Day 37

If a slave runs away from his owner and comes to you for protection, do not send him back. (Deuteronomy 23:15, GNB)

In the worst days of slavery in our own recent history, the penalties for running away were desperately severe. A recaptured slave could expect to be humiliated, beaten or even severely disabled as a punishment. By the same token, anyone who found a runaway slave would be sending him or her back to this fate.

The language of slavery is the language of ownership, reducing the slave from a human in relationship to a thing to be possessed. Deuteronomy does not challenge the institution of slavery, but invites the community to subvert it. Don't send the runaway back to face punishment.

This passage is similarly ambivalent about prostitution and capitalism. You are not to become a temple prostitute and even if you do, you are not to use the money for sacred purposes. Don't lend at interest – well, OK, but only to foreigners.

The intention of Deuteronomy is to build a community based on God's principles of justice, mercy and righteousness. Practices that seem to be endemic in the life of the people or in the cultures that surround them, cause real difficulties. The laws engage in a practical struggle with the realities of day-to-day life.

If Christian discipleship is to mean anything, then we will struggle with the same issues. What about prostitution? Is the way forward to legalise it or ban it? We still face moral dilemmas about the source and use of money as we try to work within the economic structures to encourage fair trading and ethical investment. And, for heaven's sake, what do we do about the Lottery? Economic community also raises questions about the integration of foreigners, just as it did for the Deuteronomist. All these issues are complex and interrelated. Justice and righteousness may be unclear, or even clash.

But one thing is clear. If ever you have a runaway slave in your hands, or another person in trouble, don't leave them to the harshness of an unjust system. Whatever else happens, God's gentle law says that someone who is desperate ought to be able to find protection.

God of justice and mercy, help your people to live as true disciples in this complicated world. Keep our minds lively so that we do not resort to unjust rules or rigid traditions. Keep our arms open so that people who are victims or survivors of cruelty may find protection in your strong embrace.

Day 38

A sharing community
Acts 4:32–7

No-one said that any of his belongings was his own,
but they all shared with one another
everything they had. (Acts 4:32, GNB)

Not only did they share their possessions, but more than that, they also went and sold their land and houses and gave the cash for distribution. One couple who lied about the amount they had received from the sale were struck dead on the spot!

The earliest followers of Jesus made this amazing experiment in communal living; one that has been repeated from time to time in various faith communities. It is easy to knock it, especially from the uneasy perspective of someone who owns more than she or he needs. After all, it was not long after this that Paul started writing begging letters to the Gentile churches for the poor in Jerusalem. Without the backing of owned property, the early Church's cash economy seems to have failed.

But the very experiment challenges more settled ways of life. Judaism, Marxism, and other traditions, as well as Christianity, raise questions about the nature of ownership. We have the example of nomadic cultures, which see land as a common resource, owned by none. And on our streets, the community of homeless people challenges our unthinking dependence on the ownership of property.

When the people of Israel entered the land (which had first been cleared of its indigenous inhabitants), they were given portions of land as their 'inheritance'. These portions were not owned, in the sense that they could be sold off in perpetuity. The laws of Sabbath and Jubilee rest on the ability to return to that equal sharing of property.

We are learning in our destructive times that each generation does not own the world, but holds a sacred trust for generations of people and other created beings to come. If we treat it recklessly, we may destroy what we have never owned. We are also learning how vast can be the inequities that build up if some people are allowed to own what others need in order to live.

At the heart of the Jewish Christians' experiment is a fundamental truth, a duty to share sacrificially till all need is met. All our living that falls short of that duty is theft.

God, forgive us for the arrogance in our treatment of the world in which we live, and those who share it with us. Challenge our pride in possession and undo the ties that bind us to what we own. Give us rest from ambition and greed. Relax our grasp on the world's resources so that our open hands may be filled with love.

Day 39

An easy yoke
Matthew 11:28–12:8

Come to me, all of you who are tired from carrying heavy loads, and I will give you rest. (Matthew 11:28, GNB)

God created human beings for (among other things) work and rest. The stories and poems about creation set a careful balance between them: the day for work and the night for rest, with an extra day in seven set aside solely for rest. Both are important and neither should dominate.

How good rest is! At the end of a long day's work, to put your feet up and relax. To lie down in bed and sleep away the night hours. At the weekend or on holiday, to forget about the job and relax. True rest comes when we are secure, when all our physical needs are met, and when we have time. Then, and only then, we can drop our guard and laugh and love and sleep.

But Jesus interprets even the pattern of work and rest. In his service, work is not arduous – his yoke is easy and his burden light. Putting on the yoke of Jesus is tantamount to finding rest, because Jesus is gentle and humble in spirit. No harsh arrogant taskmaster, but a fellow worker, sharing the load, recognising the humility and the dignity of labour.

And with Jesus, rest is never forced. Jesus was forever upsetting the Pharisees by breaking the Sabbath. Now he and his disciples are caught out, walking in the fields and rubbing the ears of corn in their hands to eat the grain – what more restful scene could there be! Jesus' response is, as always, that the Sabbath rules were not meant to be a straitjacket, but rather to set people free.

Distortion of the pattern is destructive. When rest is enforced by imprisonment or illness or depression, when work is harsh and unremitting, then full human life is impossible. But when richly deserved rest comes after satisfying labour, and in turn renews energy for the next day, the next week, then how good rest is!

Pause for a moment to consider when you last rested. Give thanks to God for it. Then make a pact with yourself as to when you will next have time to rest, so that you will then find refreshment in your own company and God's.

God of the seventh day, we thank you for sleep, for rest, for laughter and leisure, for time to be with friends, time to share with lovers, time to be alone, time to be with you. Jesus, help us to take up your easy yoke, lift your light burden, and gently follow you.

Day 40

PALM SUNDAY: 'I AM THE RESURRECTION AND THE LIFE'

LESLIE GRIFFITHS

John 11:17–27

Jesus said to her, 'I am the resurrection and the life.
He who believes in me will live, even though he dies;
and whoever lives and believes in me will never die.
Do you believe this?' (John 11:25–6)

These are the traditional opening words of the funeral service and many a priest or minister has recited them as he or she precedes the coffin into a church highly charged with raw emotion. Through its association with such moments and events, this declaration of Jesus too easily acquires an entirely wrong meaning. We too readily push the field of application for these words about resurrection into the mysterious realm that lies beyond our finite life. Real life, we are tempted to conclude, lies on the other side of the grave.

But is that the true meaning of this bold statement of Jesus? He has just raised Lazarus from the dead and shown how life and death overlap a great deal more than biology or logic suggest. And, within a few verses of saying these words, he'll be justifying the actions of Lazarus' sister Mary in using, and apparently wasting, expensive ointment in washing his feet. 'Couldn't this have been sold and the money given to the poor?' his critics demand. To which Jesus replies, by indicating to those present, that Mary is simply preparing his body for death. So, under that same roof, we see a dead man brought back to life and a living man being treated as if he were dead. Resurrection is to be understood far more deeply than simply the linear extension of biological life. In the midst of life there's death: that's one side of things. The other reveals how the trappings of what resembles death are charged with the rainbow colours of life itself.

Christian Aid has popularised a brilliant slogan: 'We believe in life before death'. That should help us to focus on the radical offer being made by Jesus: the offer of life, abundant life, resurrection life, which is available within the span of our mortal existence as well as beyond it. That thought should inspire and challenge all of us to work for a world where justice and peace flourish, and within which the peoples of the earth can get a life, a real life, the true life that not even death can kill.

We thank you, dear Lord, for showing us a new way of understanding our mortality; for all those glimpses of eternity, all those intimations of immortality, with which our daily lives are charged. Help us to work constantly for a world where the warmth of faith, the light of hope, and the warmth of love flourish and abound.

Day 41

A NEW EARTH

PAULA CLIFFORD

Hope through prayer
Matthew 21:14–22

If you believe, you will receive whatever
you ask for in prayer. (Matthew 21:22)

When Jesus rode into Jerusalem, the crowd welcomed him as their long-awaited Messiah. And Palm Sunday encourages us not simply to look ahead to Jesus' glorious victory in his death and resurrection, but also to his eventual return at the end of the present age. As Christians wait for his second coming, there are many reasons to hope. One of them is Jesus' promise about prayer.

The fate of the fig-tree is remarkable, in that this is the only time the Gospels record Jesus performing a 'destructive' miracle. This has led some people to suggest that verses 18–19 may reflect a saying about fruitless trees rather than an action. But what is important is that, either way, Jesus is here making a statement about faith breaking down. The Hebrew people have failed to bear fruit for God; instead, as the parable of the tenants suggests (Matthew 21:33–44), they have been trying to make themselves rich at his expense. And Jesus' action in cleansing the Temple has already shown how this has affected their prayer life as a nation.

Verse 22 is difficult, for we all know of occasions when prayer offered in faith appears to have gone unanswered. Yet in the incident of the fig-tree, Jesus is showing his disciples the ultimate power of faith in him, and in the truth he has already taught them, that everything is possible for one who believes (Mark 9:23). We need have no doubts about the truth of Jesus' promise on prayer. All that remains uncertain – to us – is the timing of its fulfilment. So the fig-tree is a dramatic example of the power of faith, and a constant encouragement to us to be faithful in prayer.

People in difficult situations are not afraid to ask God to change things in a big way. A woman from downtown Kingston, Jamaica, asked a recent visitor: 'Pray that God will help our community and change the minds of violent people who live here: pray that everyone can live in love and harmony.' As Christians, we trust God to work in the big things as well as in the small details of our personal lives.

Help us, Lord, to be faithful in prayer, both for ourselves and those close to us, and for your children across the world: for those we know, and for the millions we don't. May we commit every aspect of life, big and small, to you, constant in believing that with you everything is possible.

Day 42

Trusting in God
Psalm 31:1–8, 14–16

Into your hands I commit my spirit. (Psalm 31:5)

Psalm 31 will strike a chord with anyone who has suffered illness or distress (v. 9), who has been misunderstood by friends (v. 11), or has been in great danger (v. 13). The Psalmist has suffered much, and he does not hesitate to pour out his feelings. And the depth of emotion that he reveals is indicative of how he understands God and how much he trusts him: you don't show feelings like this to someone who is aloof or indifferent to your plight; you don't make yourself this vulnerable to someone you don't trust.

The highest degree of trust is shown in verse 5, where the Psalmist commits his life into God's hands; the verse used by Jesus as he was dying on the cross. It's a verse that has given comfort to many people at the moment of death, among them Martin Luther, whose great hymn, 'A stronghold sure our God is still', echoes the trust of the Psalmist.

Psalm 31 is a reminder that prayer is not just about seeking things from God, including apparently impossible ones. The Christian's life of prayer is one in which nothing is hidden from God, certain as we are of his 'unfailing love' (v. 16) whatever our circumstances. God is portrayed as a refuge, which is both a place where someone who is hurt can find comfort and safety, and something less concrete – an inner escape from the pressures of life.

The consequence of trusting God is that whatever happens to

them, people find in him a cause for thanksgiving. This is evident among Christians across the world who suffer poverty, oppression and disaster. A recent instance was in El Salvador in Central America. After months of serious earthquakes and tremors, in which thousands were killed or injured and many homes destroyed, Christians brought all their pain and grief to God at a service in Analabajo. One elderly lady confessed, 'We've been a bit sad and very scared . . . the tremors keep happening and it's all very stressful.' But in the service they all responded, 'The Lord's kindness has helped us through this difficult situation.'

Deepen our trust in you, O Lord our God; shelter us from the inner and outer storms of life and send us out again with new strength to follow the example of your Son and of all his people who have entrusted their lives to you. May we always rejoice in your unfailing love.

Day 43

Seeds that die
John 12:20–6

Unless a grain of wheat falls to the ground and dies,
it remains only a single seed. But if it dies it
produces many seeds. (John 12:24)

Seeds are a familiar symbol of hope, containing as they do the promise of new life and growth. For Irene, a Brazilian farmer who was thrown off her land in the 1980s, it was mango seeds. She took refuge in a camp set up by the Movement of the Landless in the grounds of a church. There she planted her seeds. When eventually, years later, she and her family were settled on their own land, in a settlement they called 'New Hope', the seeds had grown into trees and were already bearing fruit.

Jesus, though, draws attention to something we tend to overlook: that death is part of the picture too. For plants to produce seed, something has first to die. And if those seeds are to produce new life, they too have to die in the sense that they do not continue to exist as seeds. They become something different, producing life and fruit.

Jesus is clearly thinking of his own death, which is now very close. He is to die not only on behalf of his own race, but on behalf of all people. In Mark's Gospel, when he cleared the Temple of money changers, he told the people, 'My house will be called a house of prayer for all nations' (Mark 11:17). And although Jesus does not appear to meet the Greeks who come to see him, their arrival suggests that the restrictive nature of Jewish nationalism is nearly at an end. The resurrection command to preach the gospel to all nations is not far off.

Yet there is here too a veiled command to the disciples and to all of us who come after them. Proclaiming the gospel, enabling others to share in the eternal life of God's people, may not cause our physical death, but it does lead us to put our own wills and desires aside, and instead allow God to be glorified in us.

As Calvary draws closer, Jesus prepares to surrender himself completely to God. The seed has overtones of death, but out of death will come new life and, with it, new hope.

Jesus prayed: 'Father, the time has come. Glorify your Son, that your Son may glorify you.' Lord, make us more worthy of being your servants in whom you are glorified. Help us to put to death our wrong desires and to seek new life in you.

Day 44

MAUNDY THURSDAY: SERVANTS AND MASTERS

KATHY GALLOWAY

John 13:5–15

Now that I, your Lord and Teacher, have washed your feet, you also should wash one another's feet. I have set you an example that you should do as I have done for you. (John 13:14–15)

Jesus washed the feet of his disciples, an act of hospitality and courtesy. In hot and dusty Palestine, one could not be properly at ease with sweaty, dirty feet. But to Peter, it was an offence that his master should perform so menial a task. To wear a slave's garment, to get down on the floor and clean off the dirt, offended every notion of what should be offered up to holiness.

Every society has its people who it delegates to deal with its bodily dirt and they always come at the bottom of the social scale – low paid, dishonoured, sometimes destined through generations to be the ones whose very name contains our fear of mortality: the 'untouchables'. And here was Jesus doing this work. But his disciples could not deter him. This was something they had to learn: that there is no untouchable area for God. Not the sweat of human bodies, not the stink of the rubbish dump on which he died, not even the stench of decay from the grave of Lazarus. No smell bad enough to keep God away. No recoiling from corruptible human flesh.

Not even our own. Hard as it is for our society to value the servant role properly, when every transaction is an economic one, it is even more difficult for us to allow ourselves to be served, especially when the service is a bodily one. It makes us vulnerable, exposes all our weaknesses. No wonder we seek to render invisible those who serve us! In our heart of hearts, we know there is something lacking in the terms by which we negotiate the meeting of our most intimate needs. The dishonour, disgust and profound inequality we project on to others are a measure of how hard it is for us to accept our own deepest humanity, how hard it is to affirm intimacy. But Jesus modelled a different kind of giving and receiving of service, one rooted firmly on mutual acceptance, respect and love for one another in all our frailty. This embodied act of grace, more clearly than any other in Scripture, awakens, confronts, embraces and transforms our fears of loving and being loved.

> *Lord Jesus, you put a face to love.*
> *It is your face.*
> *But it is my face too.*
> *It is the face of my neighbour*
> *and the face of the stranger . . .*
> *We give thanks for those who,*
> *on our behalf,*
> *care for those aspects of our human existence*
> *we would rather forget.*
> *We pray to be like you, and them,*
> *in generosity and grace.*

Day 45

GOOD FRIDAY: THE SURPRISE OF SUFFERING

KATHY GALLOWAY

Isaiah 52:13–53:3

Like one from whom men hide their faces he was despised, and we esteemed him not. (Isaiah 53:3)

Good Friday confronts us with the raw reality of suffering. Even after 2,000 years, and the layer upon layer of interpretation, dogma, distortion and mythologising that culture, ideology and history have placed on the fact of the cross, something about a man crucified breaks through to shock.

In autumn 2000, a small South African boy called Nkosi Johnston also broke through. At an international conference on AIDS, he challenged politicians, doctors, journalists and an indifferent world genuinely to look and see the person behind the statistics and the rhetoric. When he died, the reality of his skeletal child's body told its own story of unbearable suffering, and we were shocked out of complacency.

God knows why suffering should surprise us. Crucifixion, in one form or another, is the most wearily predictable thing in the world. It is one of the few constants in life. And yet, the cancer of a loved one, the betrayal of a friend, or the sheer injustice of so many kinds of losses, still brings us to our knees in shock.

We live in a world that so often seems to value only the attractive, the productive, the exotic. Everything that does not fit the glossy picture is airbrushed out. This is not accidental. The Japanese theologian, Kosuke Koyama, writes:

What is love if it remains invisible and intangible? Those who do not love a brother or sister whom they have seen cannot love God whom they have not seen. The devastating poverty in which millions of children live is visible. Racism is visible. Machine guns are visible. Slums are visible. The gap between rich and poor is glaringly visible. Our response to these realities must be visible. Grace cannot function in a world of invisibility . . . People, because of the image of God they embody, must remain seen . . . Religion seems to raise up the invisible and despise what is visible. But it is the 'see, hear, touch' gospel that can nurture the hope which is free from deception.[10]

The crucified body of Christ is mocked if it does not make visible to us all the other crucifixions of *our* world and *our* time.

Lord Jesus,
in your own body you took upon yourself
the invisibility of all who are crucified
by war, disease, poverty, oppression and fear
and you made it visible.
When we would rather turn our faces away,
draw us by your love
and give us your courage
to confront all that denies life
and to bear witness to your living hope.

Day 46

HOLY SATURDAY: FROM THE CROSS TO RESURRECTION

JOHN GLADWIN

Hebrews 10:19–25

Let us draw near to God with a sincere heart in full assurance of faith. (Hebrews 10:22)

This is a day of rest and waiting. Our Lord's body lies in the tomb. The trauma of crucifixion is over. A sense of waiting is the meaning of the day. As the day moves on, so the confidence of the Christian grows. We begin to look forward to the opening of the tomb and the joy of resurrection. We must be patient and move with the pace of the story and of this day.

The writer of the letter to the Hebrews gives his readers a sense of movement. We enter the sanctuary by the blood of Jesus. We approach the heavenly place in full assurance of faith. We do so holding on to the hope of what is to come.

So much of our world and of our life is caught between Good Friday and Easter Day. We know the suffering and the death, and we carry the hope of something better in our hearts. Will the justice and righteousness of God be vindicated? The journey we have made in following the suffering and death of our Lord takes us into the heart of the suffering and dying of humanity. Today, with the shed blood of Jesus so close to hand, we wait in patient hope. The body lies in the quietness of the tomb – might there be a moving of the stone at its entrance?

If this gives us deep confidence that the trauma and injustice of the cross is an open door to a different future, how are we to respond and prepare? We are to provoke one another to love and good deeds – not just good deeds but action rooted in a loving heart. We are to meet together to offer one another encouragement. Those who believe in a different future and who look for new life need encouraging. Easter is the day of encouragement for all who live and work for that which is yet to come in all its fullness.

As the day of death draws to a close and the day of life opens in front, may we find hope and life for all in our broken and wounded world.

> *Lord Jesus, whose body lay in the tomb awaiting the day of resurrection, teach us to wait and work with patience for the unfolding of your justice and salvation in our dying world. Help us to enter the Day of Resurrection with hope and joy. Shape our lives in the world in love and goodness and bring encouragement to all who struggle for justice and peace.*

Day 47

EASTER SUNDAY: INTO ANOTHER COUNTRY

JOHN GLADWIN

Hebrews 13:13–21

---

*Here we do not have an enduring city, but we are
looking for the city that is to come. (Hebrews 13:14)*

We follow a Saviour who won his triumph through being
driven out of the city of the present. Like the Old Testament scapegoat, he was driven from the present to die in the
wilderness and carry the abuse of us all. There we meet him,
beyond the walls of the city, the crucified and risen Lord. It is he
who calls us out from the cities of our present to meet him in the
suffering of rejection, and find in the life that is offered a vision of
a city still to come. We are the people of the future city. This is
God's city embodied in the risen life of Jesus Christ.

As we travel this journey of faith in the Lord who died and is
now risen, so we must draw the present towards the future. Our
journey is marked by worship and praise, by persistent goodness
and sacrificial generosity, and by the disciplined life of the community. Through all we are sustained by the prayer of God's people.

Our Lord is out of the tomb. His hands and feet bear the marks
of the cross. We, who are to be his risen body in the world, must
live with the reality of suffering to draw humanity into the life of
the future. We cannot live at Easter without the oppressed and
abused of the world.

In Lent we resolved to discipline our lives by fasting, prayer
and giving. At Easter we reshape our lives to be a message of hope

for the lost and a way of justice for the rejected. Before our eyes is the vision of the city to come – a place marked by equity, life, trust, justice and peace. We live knowing that the one who was driven out of the present is the one who shapes the future. On Easter Day we renew our commitment to Jesus Christ and resolve again to be people of the future.

Hebrews gives us the words of the Easter Blessing. Ponder its beauty and humanity. Let it be a door into the heart of God and a way into renewed Christian life.

Lord God, who brought again our Lord Jesus Christ from the dead, draw us into the life of the city that is to come. Make us a beacon of hope in a dark world, a means of life for a dying humanity, and a force for justice amid oppression and abuse. May the joy of this day renew us all in your service.

Notes

1 Dalit prayer.
2 Norman Hart, in *A World of Blessing,* compiled by Geoffrey Duncan, Canterbury Press, Norwich, 2000.
3 Geiko Müller-Fahrenholz, in *The Art of Forgiveness: Theological Reflection on Healing and Reconciliation*, WCC, Geneva, 1997.
4 Peter West, 'Rwanda Return', an internal Christian Aid paper, January 2000.
5 Thomas Wilson, seventeenth-century English bishop.
6 Peter West, 'Rwanda Return'.
7 Ken Leech, *We Preach Christ Crucified: the Proclamation of the Cross in a Dark Age*, Darton, Longman & Todd, London, 1994, p. 5.
8 Deepa Narayan, Robert Chambers *et al.*, *Voices of the Poor Crying Out for Change*, Oxford University Press for the World Bank, Oxford, 2000, pp. 22–7.
9 Amanecide Collective, *Revolutionary Forgiveness: Reflections on Nicaragua*, Orbis Books, Maryknoll, 1987, p. 128.
10 Address to WCC General Assembly, Harare, 1998.